GETTING A JOB IN
THE RETAIL
INDUSTRY

LAURA LA BELLA

Published in 2017 by The Rosen Publishing Group, Inc.
29 East 21st Street, New York, NY 10010

Library of Congress Cataloging-in-Publication Data

Names: La Bella, Laura, author.
Title: Getting a job in the retail industry / Laura La Bella.
Description: First edition. | New York : Rosen Publishing, 2016. | Series:
 Job basics: getting the job you need | Includes bibliographical references
 and index.
Identifiers: LCCN 2016007642 | ISBN 9781477785584 (library bound)
Subjects: LCSH: Retail trade—Vocational guidance—Juvenile literature.
Classification: LCC HF5429.29 .L32 2016 | DDC 381/.1023—dc23
LC record available at http://lccn.loc.gov/2016007642

Manufactured in China

CONTENTS

INTRODUCTION

The retail industry is enormous. It is the largest private employer in the nation and, as a $435 billion a year industry, it is a crucial part of the American economy. Economists, the people who study the health of the economy, look to the retail industry for clues for how strong our economy is based on how much spending is happening among consumers. When people are buying goods and spending money, the economy is strong and growing.

The retail industry refers to the sale of goods from a mall, boutique store, super store, or department store directly to consumers. Think about all of the items you buy on a regular basis—food, clothing, shoes, jewelry, make-up, video games, toys, cell phones—all of those items come from stores. And those stores employ retail workers.

The retail industry employs the largest number of people in the United States—more than 29 million—that's one in four jobs. Retail workers are employed in a wide variety of retail operations that sell all kinds of goods, including furniture and home furnishings, electronics and appliances, building materials and home/garden improvement, health and personal care, clothing and shoes, jewelry and accessories, sporting goods and hobby, music and books, and more.

The people behind this mega industry are employed in retail stores that can range from large department stores, discount stores, warehouse stores, and super stores, to boutique specialty stores. They also hold a wide range of jobs.

Sales associates help customers choose clothing and other goods at retail stores. They are one part of the giant, thriving retail industry.

Retail workers are responsible for selecting the merchandise sold in stores; selling the merchandise to customers; managing store operations and store staff; designing the layout of a stores to optimize sales; designing and creating store and window displays to entice shoppers; and even act as personal shoppers for individual customers.

The retail industry is a field that does not require a college education for entry-level positions. Many positions require only a high school diploma. For those who want to pursue specialty positions, such as visual merchandisers and managers, some level of college level course work is encouraged and preferred. Retail is an industry that also provides upward mobility in the form of promotions for those that work hard and show a dedication to customer service and product knowledge. Often sales people are promoted to management positions based on their talent, skills, and aspirations.

The retail industry's range of jobs also means you can be employed full- or part-time, and as early as a teenager. Many teens work in the retail industry part-time while they attend high school and college. With flexible hours that span days, evenings, and weekends, these jobs are perfect for anyone interested in working part-time for extra money or full-time as a career option.

Surveying the Retail Field

I n every town in America, no matter its size, you can find stores. Consumers have needs and wants—groceries, clothing, sporting goods, furniture, shoes, jewelry, games, toys, electronics, books—and they fulfill them at retail locations. The retail industry is enormous in America. It accounts for one in four jobs and brings in a total of $435 billion a year. That's a lot of products that move from store shelves and into homes each and every day.

With an industry this huge, there are an abundance of jobs that need to be filled in nearly every single aspect of the retail field. Products need to be managed in a warehouse before they are moved onto trucks and delivered to individual stores. Once they arrive at stores, the products need to be stocked in the back of the store, unpacked, and prepared for display in the front of the store. Products are moved onto the selling floor where they are displayed in visually appealing, strategic ways to entice shoppers to make a purchase. Once on the selling floor, sales people with knowledge of the various products sell to consumers who have a need for a product. Products are purchased and packaged for delivery by those who work at registers and process sales transactions. Overseeing the entire operation are managers who,

The flat-screen TV you see on the floor of your local big box store had a long journey to get to its destination. Retail workers were the last stop in its journey from the manufacturer into a customer's hands.

BEST PLACES TO WORK IN RETAIL

Choosing a retail store to work at can be difficult. With thousands of choices, where do you begin to look for place that might be the right fit for you? *Fortune* magazine has published a list of top places to work in retail. Below is a selection of the best places to begin your career in the retail industry:

Build-a-Bear Workshop: A shop where children choose the type of stuffed animal they want, have it stuffed on-site, and select a range of clothing and accessories for the animal. The company treats its employees well: it delivers treats, lunches, and prizes to its hardworking store employees during the holiday season and workers can earn free stuff, like company items and small cash bonuses.

Wegmans Food Markets: Based in Rochester, N.Y., and located throughout the Northeast, Wegmans is the ultimate grocery store with a huge selection of ready-made, gourmet meals and a variety of grocery items. The company offers college scholarships to high school and college-aged employees and workers can manage their work schedules around school, family, and needed time off via an online scheduling system.

The Container Store: The place to get organized, The Container Store offers consumers all types of organization systems for home and office use. Those who are employed full-time in sales have the opportunity to make an average of $50,000 a year.

L.L. Bean: The outdoor store sells everything you need for camping, kayaking, running, hiking, and more. Company-planned excursions allow employees to experience the outdoors, and hard workers are celebrated with a parade, catered reception, and gifts. The company also owns camps and tent sites near its headquarters in Maine, which employees can use for free on a lottery system.

DSW: Short for Designer Shoe Warehouse, this discount shoe store offers career mapping to help employees develop sales skills. They also reward employees with a point system where points can be exchanged for jewelry, electronics, and furniture.

depending on the size of the store, can supervise all of these operations or just one or two of them. In large stores, there are multiple managers who work as a team and split up management duties and oversee specific responsibilities. In smaller stores, there may be one or two managers who are responsible for all of these pieces of the retail operation.

A Wide Range of Jobs

The retail industry offers a range of jobs that goes beyond sales people selling in the store. There are opportunities for you to work behind the scenes as well, such as helping select the products that will be sold; creating visual displays that entice customers to learn more abut a product and ultimately buy it; and in managing a store's operations, which can include hiring staff, developing their skills, training sales

Jobs in retail involve more than just straightforward selling. Window displays and other visual merchandising are key components of creating consumer interest in consumer goods.

Store managers lead by example and provide guidance to their sales staffs. They also serve as a liaison to a store's owner, whether they are locally owned or part of a corporation, and help achieve a store's overall goals.

people and other personnel on customer service skills, and managing the day-to-day operations of a retail operation.

What are some jobs in retail that go beyond the sales person?

• **Store managers:** These retail professionals are responsible for the daily operations of a store. They offer exemplary customer service, problem solve for customers, handle business operations, and work to meet sales goals for the store.

• **Buyers:** Have you ever wondered how products are selected for sale in your favorite store? This is the job of a buyer. A buyer is responsible for selecting and purchasing new products that, based on marketing information, they think will sell well in a given store or geographic location.

• **Merchandisers:** These sales professionals know their consumers and can predict which products will be best sellers. They help decide

Product displays should be well thought out to help customers easily find the items they need, as well be visually enticing and pleasant to look at.

which promotional events will happen and when, and they help a store and its management meet their sales goals.

• **Visual merchandisers:** Product displays are not random and they aren't thought up on the spot. Visual merchandisers, who study consumer behavior, buying behavior, and how visual cues can impact a consumer's decision to buy a product, create these displays. Visual merchandisers consider the individual product, the type of consumer that regularly shops in a particular store, as well as physical space and lighting to create a display that draws attention and pulls people into a store to learn more.

• **Logistics:** People who work in logistics figure out how products are getting from the manufacturer to the warehouse to the store and to people's homes. They are responsible for distributing and transporting products in the fastest, most economical ways possible.

Opportunities Abound

The sheer size of the retail industry means that opportunities are available for full- and part-time work, as well as seasonal positions for high volume shopping periods, such as summer or holidays. And, with so many stores to choose from, you can work with products you like and personally enjoy.

Are you stylish and interested in fashion? A clothing store may be the perfect fit for you as you learn about the latest trends and help consumers choose the latest styles. Are you an expert gamer? As a sales person for a gaming store, your knowledge of gaming and gaming consoles can be immeasurable as you provide expert consultation on which system is best for a customer's needs.

Are you a sports enthusiast? Sporting good stores are a perfect place for you to share your knowledge of sports, sporting equipment and recreation. The opportunity for you to work in an area of retail that matches up with a personal interest is outstanding.

Retail is a career field that can provide you with a number of employment options that meet your personal or career aspirations. You may not be interested in a permanent career in retail, but rather a way to earn extra money. You can work part-time to earn extra income while you finish high school, or as you work your way through college. For those who are interested in a permanent, full-time career, you can work full-time as you gain experience in sales, customer service, management, or merchandising. And, with hard work and a solid work ethic, opportunities to be promoted to positions of management and leadership give you a chance to grow within a retail company and aim for positions that offer you more responsibility.

CHAPTER TWO

What Retail Workers Do

Retail jobs can vary greatly and can include a wide range of duties, responsibilities, educational requirements, and opportunities for success.

Store Clerks/Sales Associates

Store clerks, who are often called sales people or sales associates, sell merchandise, such as clothing, furniture, shoes, and jewelry to customers in need. They help consumers find the items they need, offer guidance on fit, style, and selection of items, and they process customers' payments.

Duties and Responsibilities

The daily duties and responsibilities of a store clerk include any of the following activities: greeting customers when they arrive in the store and offering them assistance, making recommendations on merchandise, explaining the use and benefits of merchandise to customers, answering customers' questions, demonstrating how merchandise works (such as a small appliance), processing customers' orders, and informing customers of any sales, promotions, incentives, and policies on payment and returns/exchanges.

Work Environment

Retail sales clerks work in stores. These locations are well-lit, clean, and located in areas where there is consistent consumer traffic for sales. Sales clerks should be physically fit, as most stand for long periods of time and walk continually throughout a store assisting consumers. For sales clerks that work in home improvement stores or garden stores, you may work outside in all types of weather conditions. Retail workers work long hours and usually work evenings, weekends, and holidays. Some times of the year, such as peak times during holiday shopping or end-of-the-year sales, you may not be able to take vacation time due to the increase in consumer shopping and the need for more store clerks to be scheduled to handle the crowds.

Academic or Training Requirements

Sales clerk positions require no formal educational requirements.

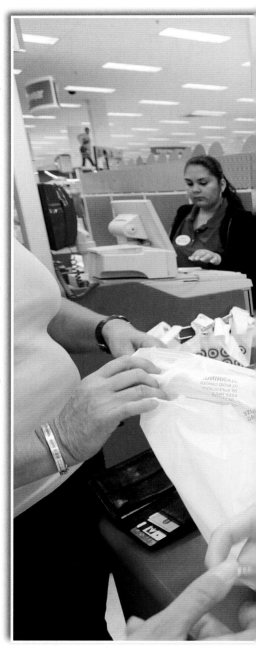

Educational requirements vary for jobs in the retail industry. However, entry level sales positions can be filled by students who are still in high school. With experience, these jobs can lead to management roles.

Some employers prefer applicants to have a high school diploma or be working toward one. Most sales clerks are provided on-the-job training by the store. This training can include customer service and care, looking out for and preventing loss prevention (also called shoplifting), understanding the store's policies and procedures, and instructions on operating the cash register to process sales, returns, or exchanges.

Depending on what the sales clerk is selling, sometimes more in depth training is provided to the sales clerk. This training might be appropriate for technical products such as computers or smartphones, high-end jewelry, furniture, or cosmetics.

Store/Retail Manager

Store or retail managers are responsible for the daily operations of a store. They lead by example as they handle interactions with customers and staff.

Store managers are responsible for day-to-day store operations as well as developing their sales staff through training and leadership. Here, a manager inspects her subordinate's paperwork.

Store window displays that are creative and exciting distinguish stores from their competitors and attract customers. Visual merchandisers can really get creative when developing holiday displays.

Duties and Responsibilities

The daily duties and responsibilities of a store/retail manager include any of the following activities: recruiting, training, supervising, and appraising staff; managing budgets; maintaining the financial records of the store; promoting and marketing the business either independently or in line with corporate guidance if the store is owned by a larger company; dealing with customer in queries, complaints, and questions; overseeing store stock; coaching their team to meet sales goals; complying with local and state health and safety legislation; and preparing promotional materials and displays to announce sales and promotions.

Work Environment

Retail/store managers work in all types of stores—from small boutique stores to large superstores and in between. Store/retail managers are most often on their feet and work on the sales floor assisting sales clerks with purchases, providing customer service and care, and managing the daily operations of the store. Store/retail managers often have an office in the store, where they can make calls to store leadership (if the store is part of a larger chain) and complete paperwork.

Like retail workers, store/retail managers work long hours, including evenings, weekends, and holidays. Managers are limited in their ability to take any vacation time during high-traffic times of the year, such as around the holiday selling season and during end-of-year sales events.

Academic or Training Requirements

To become a store/retail manager, a bachelor's degree is often a requirement. Degrees in business, fashion merchandising, or management are often most beneficial. It is possible to be promoted to a manager position from a sales position without a degree.

Visual Merchandiser

This job used to be called window dresser, but today, people who design window displays and arrange product displays throughout the store are called visual merchandisers.

Duties and Responsibilities

The daily duties and responsibilities of a visual merchandiser include any of the following activities: creating design ideas for store displays and developing floor plans for the strategic positioning of merchandise; coordinating the placement of new merchandise on the selling floor; creating special displays to promote specific products or special offers; developing

IMPORTANT QUALITIES FOR EMPLOYEES IN RETAIL JOBS

Those who succeed in retail jobs like to be around other people, find helping others rewarding, and enjoy sales and selling. There are key qualities that are important for people to possess if they are pursuing a career in retail.

- *Customer-service skills*: You will work with people consistently. Being attentive and responsive to customer's wants and needs is important. You should be able to ascertain what a customer is looking for, know the products you have available to sell, and even be aware of alternatives should they ask for further suggestions.
- *Interpersonal skills*: These are the skills we use each day as we communicate and interact with other people. Interpersonal skills include verbal and nonverbal communication, listening, problem solving, decision-making, and assertiveness. As a sales clerk, communicating with others is essential. You need to be able to seek out what a consumer is looking for and why. To do this you must be able to listen to their needs and wants, seek out nonverbal clues as to how they are feeling, provide solutions to their problems, and be assertive in offering suggestions and recommendations. You must also be able to explain how a product works, or why the product you are selling is better than the competitors'.
- *Math skills*: As a sales clerk, you must be able to calculate a total for a purchase, how much a discount comes to on merchandise, and compute change owed to customers.
- *Persistence*: Sometimes consumers are just browsing and not interested in shopping. Your attempts to sell merchandise may be unsuccessful. Persistence is when you continue to pursue sales even if you are unsuccessful with your previous customer.
- *Salesmanship*: There is a difference between providing information about a product and selling a product. Selling skills include being persuasive while you are providing product information.

in-store displays and visuals; deciding how to use the store's space and its lighting creatively; making best use of a store's available floor space and layout; setting up displays using merchandise from the store; dressing mannequins and arranging displays in windows and in other areas of the store; instructing and training sales staff how products should be displayed and how often they should be changed; and removing old displays.

Work Environment

Visual merchandisers work in all types of stores, and can be responsible for creating the visual displays for clothing, furniture, beauty items, shoes, and even electronics. These jobs often require you to be able to carry heavy merchandise or display structures (such as shelving and mannequins), boxes and accessories around the

A merchandise buyer is in charge of selecting which products will sell and in which environment. They base their decisions on buyer behavior, marketing research, and product knowledge.

selling floor for set up. You will also be on your feet most days. It can be a physically demanding job. For those that work for a chain of stores, you may be responsible for the visual display in several locations and some travel may be required.

Academic or Training Requirements

Visual merchandisers often need an associate degree in fashion or visual merchandising, plus two to four years of experience working in a retail environment. Some positions may require you to submit a portfolio that shows your past work through a collection of photographs and illustrations you have created for a particular store.

Merchandise Buyer

A merchandise buyer is responsible for selecting the products that will be for sale in a particular store, catalog, or consumer website. A buyer needs to understand who the consumer is and what their interests are to best select the type of merchandise that will sell well in a particular type of store. They even need to have a clear understanding of the local or regional culture for a specific geographic location, as buying behavior if often different is varying parts of the country. For example, winter coats will need to be available in abundance in clothing stores in the northeast from early fall through mid-winter. However, in the southwest, winter coats are not necessary for the weather conditions and lightweight outerwear is more appropriate. A buyer needs to understand the needs of their consumers and plan accordingly.

Duties and Responsibilities

The daily duties and responsibilities of a merchandise buyer include any of the following activities: buying merchandise for their area(s) of responsibility; working alongside other staff to select product themes and the vendors who can supply the materials/products needed; understanding the customer's profile; anticipating consumer buying behavior using market data, competitive shopping analysis, and current business trends; negotiating purchases and delivery dates with vendors; and supervising assistant buyers and other buying staff.

Work Environment

Depending on the size and number of stores, a merchandise buyer can work either at a company's corporate headquarters for a company that owns a chain of stores or they may work at one store if it is privately owned. Sometimes private store owners act as the buyer for their own businesses.

Academic or Training Requirements

Merchandise buyers often need several years of experience working in a retail operation, or a combination of experience and an associate or bachelor's degree. They should also possess negotiation skills for dealing with vendors, organizational skills for managing multiple vendors and merchandise orders, as well as strong customer service skills. On-the-job training can often include training in the policies and procedures specific to a large company and computer training for specific types of programs or software associated with buying merchandise and tracking sales.

Duties and Responsibilities

The daily duties and responsibilities of a merchandise buyer include any of the following activities: building a client base of loyal shoppers who are seeking your advice on style and clothing purchases; creating a personal shopping experience for a client, which can include bringing clothing items to their home for personal wardrobing; negotiating sales for clients for high-end, exclusive items; and keeping clients informed of changing trends and styles.

Personal Shoppers

For people who want a personal, customized shopping experience, a personal shopper is the person you turn to. These shopping professionals provide advice on style and wardrobe choices to maximize current style trends. They provide personal customer service by selecting clothing items for their clients that meet each client's personal or professional needs. They also provide advice on the fit of clothing and on the accessories that can enhance an outfit, such as shoes, jewelry, and handbags.

Work Environment

Personal shoppers often keep a home office to communicate regularly with their clients and to keep track of changing styles and trends via Internet research and through clothing and style magazines. Most personal shoppers visit clients in the client's home and/or accompany a client to stores for a personal shopping experience. Many personal shoppers also bring clothing items to client's homes for a personal style session, where clients try on clothes and review or update the contents of the closets. Personal shoppers own their own businesses so they can determine the hours they work or how often they want to work. However many are on-call and may need to attend to a client's needs on short notice.

Academic or Training Requirements

There are no educational requirements needed to become a personal shopper; however, a deep commitment and love for fashion, accessories, shoes, and other items is needed, as is a dedication to staying current on fashion trends. Many personal shoppers have prior retail experience working in luxury or high-end clothing stores.

CHAPTER THREE

Education and Training

M any jobs in the retail industry do not require any academic study beyond a high school diploma. However, there are ways you can prepare yourself for jobs in the retail industry at all levels of academic study.

You can prepare yourself for a job in the retail industry in a number of ways. Through high school courses, classes at vocational/technical schools, courses at trade/community colleges, and four-year degree programs at the college level, you can acquire the skills and knowledge you need to succeed in retail.

High School Courses to Take

High school students who are interested in pursuing full- or part-time employment in the retail industry can take the following courses to help prepare them for the day-to-day operations of working for a retail business:

- Economics: This is the study of the various factors that determine the production, distribution, and consumption of goods and services.
- Math: Skills in adding, subtracting, and calculating sales tax and discounts are vital to people working in retail.

Math skills are important for those in retail sales. This includes cashiers and entry-level employees, as well as management.

- Marketing: The communication between a corporation and its consumers, marketing is how people learn about new products and services, and the benefits of one product over another.
- Business administration: The process of managing and operating a business, from sales, staffing decisions, and products to setting goals and organizing resources
- Sales: The act of selling a product to someone is more than just making items available for purchase. Sales is actively seeking out customers, offering them solutions to their needs, and fulfilling their wants.
- Management: People are a retail operation's greatest resources and managing them takes skill. Management is the planning and execution of business decisions to reach a company's goals.

Vocational Programs

Vocational programs include roughly 200–300 hours of class work where students learn technical skills in a specific field of study. Courses range in duration, but most are five hours or shorter. Vocational programs are offered online and on-site at vocational schools and vocational high schools. Vocational programs often do not have any admission requirements.

Vocational programs that are offered at high schools allow students to complete courses in addition to their regular high school course work. These programs prepare students for vocations after high school that do not require a college degree. Vocational programs that apply to the retail industry include business administration, hospitality, marketing and sales, and fashion merchandising.

ESTABLISH GOOD STUDY HABITS

Good study habits are essential if you want to succeed in school. Whether you're taking a high school class in retail management, working toward a vocational certificate in retail operations, or you're completing a bachelor's degree in business administration, learning how to study and how best to learn information is essential to getting good grades and to making the most of your educational experience.

Take good notes: Keep a notebook for each course you are taking and jot down notes from lectures and presentations given by your teachers. Make sure to write down the key points a professor is making about a topic.

Get and stay organized: Time management and organization are keys to handling your day-to-day responsibilities. Keep an up-to-date calendar of important events, such as tests and quizzes, plus a list of assignments and their due dates. This will help keep you on track and enable you to priorities what needs to get done first.

Disconnect: With the Internet, social media, and smartphones, we're more connected to one another than we ever have been. But all this connection can be distracting when you have studying that needs to get done and assignments to work on. Limit your activity online and on your phone during your study times so that you can focus on your assignments and get work done.

Avoid cramming for the big test: It's tempting to stay up the night before a big test and cram all of the information you need into your brain. But this tends to be counteractive. You retain less information and you will also be tired for the exam—which means you won't pay as close attention and you may make costly mistakes. Set a study schedule for yourself to follow each week so you can pace yourself and study a bit each day.

Find a place to study: Some students like the library, others prefer the lounge in their residence hall. Wherever you find the ideal place to study—which means a quiet location with few distractions and good lighting—make it your own. Study there regularly so your mind gets into its study zone and you're mentally prepared to get to work.

Take breaks: Studying for hours on end is difficult and can be exhausting. Take a ten-minute break every hour or so to stretch your body, walk around, get a drink of water, and give your mind a break from all the information.

The types of courses you will complete will vary depending on the subject matter you choose, but in general you will take courses that provide you with an overview of a career field and an introduction to the basic foundation of knowledge you will need to work in that field.

For example, at the Connecticut Technical High School, students who choose the Marketing, Sales, and Service cluster can choose a concentration in Fashion Merchandising and Entrepreneurship. According to the school's website, the cluster "provides students with the theoretical knowledge and skills for career in planning, managing, and performing marketing activities to reach organizational objectives such as brand management, professional sales, merchandising, marketing communications, and market research." Within the Fashion Merchandising and Entrepreneurship concentration, students complete four courses that provide an introduction to the world of fashion, its importance throughout history, the manufacturing process of how clothes and accessories are made, the economic impact of the fashion industry, the various business models used in the industry (direct to consumer, business-to-business, and more), the principles of management and leadership, business planning, customer service, franchising, sales promotions, sales events, visual merchandising and display, managing the back of the store and its stock, and more.

Trade/Community College Courses

Trade schools and community colleges offer course work that can lead to a certificate or a two-year associate degree in a topic related to fashion and retail, such as fashion merchandising, business, management, marketing, or organizational management, for example.

A certificate program is a set of four to eight college-level courses that provide students with a foundation in the topic area they are studying. Certificates often lead to entry-level positions within a particular industry and are often skill-based programs, meaning you are learning a specific skill set—computer programming, costume design and production, or fashion alterations—for example. These courses can often be transferred to a degree program at a later date

Vocational courses in marketing, merchandising, and other retail-connected offerings attract creative, positive, and confident candidates from many backgrounds.

and may possibly count toward an associate degree or bachelor's degree.

The fashion alterations certificate, for example, includes courses such as alteration of ready made garments, sewing with knits, advanced clothing construction, textiles, and couture sewing. These courses prepare you for jobs as a seamstress or alterations specialists at a clothing store or to open your own business where you provide clothing alteration services.

An associate degree is a two-year program, or a minimum of sixty credit hours of study in a specific program of study. Students who study fulltime will take five courses each semester for two years. These courses include general education courses in mathematics, science, and the liberal arts in addition to courses in your area of study. For example, an associate degree in fashion merchandising and design includes courses such as textiles, apparel quality analysis,

Graduates of fashion marketing or related programs have a head start when it comes to getting coveted jobs in high-end retail. In these jobs, good customer service skills can translate into lucrative commissions.

display and visual merchandising, fashion retail merchandising, retail buying, sales management, accounting and marketing, plus general education courses such as human

Your working environment can vary greatly in the retail industry. Big box stores, like Target, specialty clothing retailers like Ann Taylor, and privately owned small businesses, such as hardware stores, each provide a different working experience.

communication, composition, sciences courses and mathematics courses. An associate degree can prepare you for management positions in retail, or for more specific positions

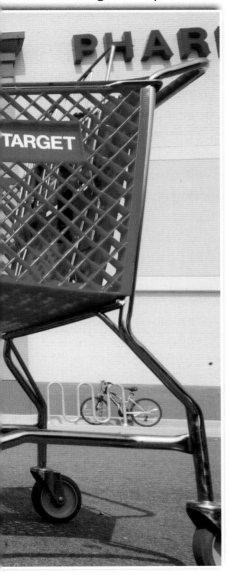

such as visual merchandiser or sales leader.

Two-year degree programs and certificate programs often have some basic admission requirements, which include a high school diploma or GED, transcripts from any previously completed college-level courses, and an application for enrollment.

Four-Year Degree Programs

For students who wish to advance in positions of management and leadership, or who may want to open their own retail establishment, a four year bachelor's degree can provide you with the advanced education you need to pursue management level positions in corporate retail companies. Majors can include business administration, fashion merchandising, marketing, management, retail management, and sales and sales management. These programs are often 120 to

140 credit hours and take four years of full-time study to complete. Students can pursue these programs on a part-time basis as well if they are balancing a job and their education. The curriculum for these programs includes specific courses that pertain to your major, plus general education courses that provide an overall education.

A bachelor's degree in retail management, for example, may include courses in retail strategy, principles and theory of management, strategic management, retail innovation, retail operations, merchandising operations, consumer behavior, supply chain management, organizational behavior, and human resource management. In addition, you will complete general education courses so you are well rounded in your education. These courses include history, social sciences (economics or sociology, for example), mathematics, sciences, and liberal arts courses such as writing, literature, composition, and public speaking.

Admission requirements vary for four-year programs based on the program and school you choose to attend. At minimum an applicant needs to have a specific high school grade point average, and have completed courses in math, science, English, and social studies.

The Job Search

Searching for a job can be an exciting time in your life. You're about to embark on a new professional experience where you will meet new people and gain new skills. You'll want to carve out time to conduct your job search and you'll want to take advantage of a variety of methods to find all the open positions you are qualified for.

Where to Start Your Search

For open positions in the retail industry, one of the best places to look is in actual stores. Walk around the mall, visit large superstores and go to box stores and look for signs announcing that the store is hiring. Most stores will post signs in their windows or large posters in their entrances announcing open positions. You can also ask to speak to a manager to learn if a store is hiring or will be posting open positions soon.

In addition to visiting actual stores, there are other resources you can utilize to identify open positions in the retail industry.

- *Public library:* Your local library has computer stations with Internet access and job databases that you can access to learn about any positions open in the retail industry. You can also research each store, the products they sell, where they are located, and more.

- *Job help centers and employment offices/services*: These services can help you identify open positions and even help you prepare your application materials, such as your resume or cover letter.
- *Job fairs*: Many communities offer job fairs throughout the year. At these events, employers attend to provide information about available openings. They may also collect resumes and conduct initial interviews.
- *Online searches*: The Internet is among the best places to search for open jobs. Job and career building websites, such as Monster.com or Indeed.com allow you to search a large geographic area for open retail positions. You can even apply online by uploading your resume and cover letter. You'll also want to search the websites of the stores you are interested in working for. Most have employment sections that provide information about open positions, what its like working for the company and corporate information about hiring policies and more.

Applying for Jobs

When applying for a job there are a few items you'll need to prepare that will help you present your skills and abilities to future employers. These include a resume and a cover letter.

Resumes

A resume is a one to two page document that highlights your professional employment, educational background, skills, and abilities. Your resume needs to be well written and organized so that hiring managers can easily understand your experience, and when and where it took place.

There are places you can turn to for assistance in writing your resume. These can include the career services offices of vocational schools, community colleges, and four-year colleges and universities; professional writers who specialized in

Retail is one industry where you will consistently see signs announcing job openings in store windows. When looking for jobs, doing a walkthrough of a nearby mall or shopping district is always a great idea.

Career fairs are a one-stop shopping experience for a job. Employers gather in one place and you get to walk around and stop at booths to learn more, distribute your resume, and network with hiring managers.

resume writing; and local employment offices. All of these places have staff specifically training in resume writing. They can help you organize your information to craft a resume that highlights the best of your abilities. The sections of your resume should include:

• *Contact information:* List your name, address, phone number, and email address.

• *Objective:* This is a one to two sentence summary of the retail position you are seeking.

• *Education:* Highlight your educational experience, which includes any college courses you have completed or degrees you have earned, where (the educational institution) you earned them, and the program or major you studied. If you were in any clubs or organizations that are related to the retail industry, you should list that involvement too.

- *Experience:* This section shows off all of your professional experience, whether it was paid or voluntary (such as internships). List the name of the company you worked for, how long you were employed, and in what position. Then, using bullets, list your specific responsibilities and accomplishments.
- *Additional skills:* This is where you can tout your computer skills, any additional languages you speak, your community involvement, and any leadership experience you have to offer.

Cover Letter Tips

The dreaded cover letter: You search online for samples to get ideas and you wonder if you're doing it right. Here are some tips on what do highlight and what to avoid when drafting your cover letter.

Don't restate your resume: Your resume is a snapshot of your professional achievements, in bullet form, that provides a hiring manager an overall look at your professional life and successes. Your cover letter gives you a chance to describe these achievements in more detail and to expand on points in your resume.

Highlight what you can offer the company: You're talented and you're an asset to any organization. Use your cover letter to tell what you bring to the table and how your skills can help the company succeed.

List your educational background: Space in a cover letter is limited, so skip the stuff they can easily see on your resume and focus on your work experience.

Customize your cover letter for each job opening: Hiring managers can tell when you've used a form letter as your cover letter, so make it personal. Take the time to write new cover letters for all of your applications, use the actual hiring manager's name, and focus on including facts about the company and specifically how your skills meet their needs.

Your resume is the one document you need in order to show off your experience, education, and related skills. Here, a job seeker gets a free resume printed as part of a one-day promotion at FedEx Kinko's in Chicago, Illinois.

Proofread: Have someone else read your cover letter to make sure you catch any grammatical or spelling errors.

Writing a Cover Letter

Your cover letter is the first impression you'll make on a hiring manager. This document is a one to two page letter that you use to introduce yourself and provide the hiring manager more in-depth information about your skills. It's just as important as your resume and should be given just as much preparation and thought.

LinkedIn, a social network focusing on professional networking, is perfect for making connections to people in different kinds of industries and a great way to publicize your skills and abilities.

THE INTERNET: YOUR JOB SEARCH PARTNER

The Internet is a powerful instrument in your job search toolkit. You can search for open positions in nearly every industry, research companies, find samples of resumes and cover letter to use as a guide, and post your resume on job search websites to let people find you. With social sites like LinkedIn, you can even connect to potential employers and network with those in your field of interest. Use these strategies to take advantage of all the Internet has to offer:

- *Search yourself:* There is such a thing as bad publicity. Hiring managers are known to search for your social media profile on the Internet, so you need to check what you've put out there. If you've posted inappropriate photos of yourself, made controversial opinions or comments, or have participated in offensive events, you may be setting yourself up for employment problems. Before you start sending out resumes review your social media presence and remove anything that could harm your chances of getting an interview or job offer.
- *Become Your Own Publicist:* LinkedIn, Facebook and other social media sites give you an opportunity to promote yourself and your achievements. Update your social media profiles to drive traffic to your personal website where you can promote your achievements, successes and awards.
- *Network:* Use LinkedIn or other professional online networks to reach out to professionals in the retail industry field. Build contacts, seek advice, or ask a seasoned professional to mentor you. You can also ask former employers to post recommendations and comments about your job skill and abilities.
- *Be Strategic with Online Applications:* Just because a website lets you upload your resume doesn't mean you should. Carefully choose where you want your resume posted and make sure it's on industry websites that benefit you the most.

Cover letters can reveal your work ethic and your attention to detail. They also provide a glimpse into your personality, which your resume often can't. A cover letter should never be a form letter that you copy and attach to all of your resumes. Instead, each job application should have its own cover letter that is tailored to the job you are seeking. If you do this, you can speak directly to why your skills are applicable to a particular position and what you can offer that company.

Preparing for the Interview

Now that you've identified and applied to open positions in the retail industry, preparing for the interview is the next step in the process. Your resume is a great snapshot of your experience and the various skills you can bring to an employer, but it doesn't tell an employer what your personality is like or how well you might connect with customers in their stores. The interview is your opportunity to highlight your abilities, education, and experience and to learn more about the company you may be working for in the future.

An interview is more than a discussion about your abilities. It's a chance for you to learn about the store, its parent company (if it's part of a corporation) and the day-to-day environment in which you'll be working. An interviewer will ask you a lot of questions about your abilities and experience.

An interview is also a chance for you to learn about the company's culture. How well do they treat their employees? If you'll work on commission is the culture competitive or supportive? Are their opportunities for you to accept more responsibility and advance through promotions? Do they provide training?

The answers to these questions will tell you a lot about the company and what it will be like to work there day in and day out. As an applicant, you should be interested if a particular store is right for you. The interview is the best way to learn more about the job, the people you'll be working with, and the environment you'll be working in.

TIPS FOR A SUCCESSFUL INTERVIEW

- *Learn more*: The interview is a chance for you to ask about the store, the company, and its products. But you should know at least the basics about the company before going into the interview. Research the store, what it sells, and to whom. Then, think about your resume and your experience so you can ask specific questions during the interview. This shows you are invested in the opportunity and interested in learning more about how you fit in with the company.
- *Make eye contact*: While you're talking with the interviewer, make direct eye contact. If you're going to be working in sales, this is especially important. As a sales person, you'll be talking to strangers and asking them how you can assist them. Eye contact is essential to making a connection with a customer and building a relationship.
- *Never speak negatively about past employers*: Not every job is perfect, and you won't like all of your bosses. The interview is not the time to speak negatively about past employers. It can portray you as immature, vindictive, and unprofessional.
- *Remember to listen:* An interview is a conversation, so you should be listening to what the other person is saying, not just thinking about what you're response is going to be. Be engaged in the conversation. Ask follow-up questions. Listen to what your interviewer is telling you about the company.

Before the Interview

Interviews are as much about sharing your skills and abilities as they are about making a good impression. During the interview, applicants should always act professionally: turn off your cell phone, leave gum and mints at home, do not bring drinks into the interview, and dress professionally.

In retail, the culture of a particular store can dictate the type of clothing you will be allowed to wear and how accepted a particular personal look may be. Depending on the store you are interviewing with and its consumer base, you may

Preparing for an interview is about more than what you wear, though you should be dressed professionally. Tailor your appearance to what current employees are wearing, especially at high-end retailers.

want to consider covering any visible tattoos, toning down wild hairstyles or hair colors, and removing body piercings. These can be acceptable forms of expression at some retailers, but at more conservative companies or if a store has a more conservative clientele, they may be improper or even seen as offensive. You don't want your personal style choices to influence an employer's decision about your ability to do the job.

On the day of your interview, plan to arrive early. You'll also want to set aside more time if you are unsure of the store's location, if you live in a community known for heavy traffic and delays, or if you're interviewing at a large mall where it can take time to get from a parking lot to the actual store. If it's possible, drive to the location a day or two ahead of time to map out where you'll park and how to get into the building. You don't want to be late, so plan accordingly.

Common Interview Questions

Many interviews begin with some common questions. These allow you to get to know the interviewer, so they can get to know you and you can begin to feel more relaxed about the conversation. How you answer these questions helps an interviewer understand who you are, what your personality is like, and if you'll fit into the store and its environment. These are eight of the most common interviewing questions and tips for the most effective ways to answer them:

Q: Tell me a little about yourself.

A: This is not a question about your life story, so leave details about where and when you were born and instead

Interviewing is an opportunity for you to learn more about a company and what the job has to offer you. Does the job come with benefits? Can you expect to be promoted? These are some of the questions you should be asking.

focus on your education, career aspirations, and why you want to work in retail.

Q: Tell me what you know about our store/products/company/brand.

A: These questions are often tests to see if you conducted any research beforehand about the company. You should know some the basic information about the store and its products, and its customers. What are their best sellers? Who are their biggest consumers (teens, adults, gamers, computer geeks)? Knowing a little about the store, its products, or its consumers can show how interested you are in the job and how well you might fit in with the store's other employees.

Q: What relevant experience do you have?

A: Your experience is more than just where you have worked before. It's a culmination of your paid work experience, internships you may have completed as part of your educational preparation, and projects and assignments you completed in your courses that are related to retail. These are all topics you can talk about when asked about your experience.

Q: What's your greatest strength?

A: This is a great place to talk about what you think you excel at. Are you great with people? Do you find it rewarding to style someone in the latest fashions? Are you knowledgeable about gaming and gaming systems? This is when you can really boast about what you have to offer your potential employer This question is really asking you why are you a great employee. If you thrive under pressure, are great at customer service, take initiative and are always looking for

Make sure to exude a positive attitude and confidence, and be friendly. Not only do these things tell your employer you will be pleasant to work with, but they also provide a clue as to how you will interact with customers.

ways to grow, pay close attention to details, and can anticipate someone's needs, tell them.

Q: What's your biggest weakness?

A: Never tell your interviewer an actual weakness. Avoid saying things like: "I'm always late to work" or "I can never keep a job." The strategy in answering this question is to answer by sharing a positive weakness. A positive weakness can include being a perfectionist or being too committed to your job.

Q: Are you good at working in a team?

A: Always answer "YES" to this question. No matter where you work, you'll work with others and there will be times when you'll need to complete a project together. This is also an opportunity to talk about your leadership skills— mention sports teams where you served as a captain, clubs were you served in a leadership role, or times when you've led class projects to positive results.

Q: Do you have any questions to ask me?

A: This is an opportunity for you to ask questions to learn more about the store, its products, where you'll be working, any benefits to employment, or any other information you'd like to know. This information will become helpful as you decide if you want to work for the retail operation you are interviewing with.

After the Interview

The interview isn't over until you have said good-bye and you're on your way home. So, be courteous, thank the interviewer for his or her time, and shake hands. Upon getting home, write a handwritten thank-you note and drop it in the mail.

A handwritten note is a personal touch that, in this age of texts and emails, is a nice touch that shows extra effort on your part. While it may have no effect on whether you get the job, it does show your interviewer that you are professional and courteous and can follow through—all key areas in retail sales and customer service.

If You Don't Get the Job

No matter how well you interviewed you may not be the right person for the job and you may not get a job offer. If this is the case, continue to seek out open positions, apply to those that interest you, and practice your interviewing skills so you can be prepared for the next interview that comes your way.

There is a lot of turn over in retail, which means people come and go regularly, so you never know when a new job might open up. Stay positive and keep looking for new opportunities to learn as you seek out a new position.

The First Day and Beyond

Congratulations, you've been offered a job in retail. Now the real work begins. You may be wondering what to expect on the first day of you new job. Often, the first day is filled with paperwork you need to complete for human resources so you can become officially employed, get paid, have taxes taken out of your paycheck, and more. You'll meet some of the other retail staff on your first day, including your supervisor and other management personnel, and you may begin with an orientation to the store or to the store's products. The first day is exciting and you'll be ready to jump in, just remember these tips:

- *Pace yourself:* You're excited and you want to make a good impression. You'll have time to do both, so pace yourself and get oriented to the new job. No company expects perfection on the first day. There will be a lot to learn, from the responsibilities of your new position and learning about products to technical training like how to operate the cash register.
- *Ask questions and keep an open mind:* You can do the job, that's why they hired you, but don't appear to have

NEW HIRE PAPERWORK

When you accept a job you'll complete a number of forms before you can begin work, such as:

- Federal and state tax documents, such as W-2 withholding and I-9 forms: These are usually completed on the first day or within the first week, and determine how much take-home pay you will receive, and how much will go to the federal, state, and local tax authorities every pay cycle.
- Health insurance forms: If you are lucky enough to receive some kind of employee subsidies toward a health insurance plan, you will likely be offered a choice of plans. Make sure you get a detailed rundown of what benefits are offered, and that securing your own insurance on the side might not be a better option. For many entry-level retail jobs, insurance can be a welcome benefit.
- Disability insurance forms: These are standard forms that give you information about your rights in case you are injured on the job.
- Personal information forms: You will be asked for contact information for family, relatives, or significant others, who may be contacted in case of an emergency.

You may also receive special manuals or handbooks that outline corporate policies and procedures, including but not limited to:

- Employee Handbook: Many retailers, especially those that are part of large corporations, have very detailed and sometimes long employee handbooks that give you specific rules you must follow if you want to stay employed there.
- Dress code: A dress code at a retailer might be more restricitve than at other jobs. Make sure to read up on what not to wear.
- Sexual harassment and liability related documentation
- Non-disclosure agreements: As an employee, you may find out about product launches and promotions early, and other information. In some cases, revealing such information can negatively and seriously impact your employers. Such agreements ensure that you will not share information, especially with competitors.

Your new job is an opportunity to gain valuable work experience, develop new skills, learn a new industry, and meet new and exciting people. Even if you are starting an entry-level position, remember: the sky's the limit if you apply yourself.

all the answers and make suggestions on how best to do things. You're part of a team now and you should seek out information on how the store operates. You should also keep an open mind, listen during training, ask questions about how things are done, and learn a store's internal processes.

•   *Make friends with an experienced employee:* Someone who has worked in retail and at your store can be helpful to you as you learn note only the store's way of doing things, but also the internal politics. They can also show you around, introduce you to people you should know (and ones you shouldn't trust), and help you understand the culture of the company.

•   *Associate with the right people:* You'll want to get along with everyone and be a team player for your store, but you'll also want to associate with the right people. Those are the staff members who work hard, have good relationships with managers, and are supportive of one another.

•   *It's OK to make mistakes:* You're new, mistakes will happen. But how you handle a mistake speaks to your integrity and character. Don't hide a mistake, take ownership and learn from the experience.

Additional Training

On your first day, or shortly afterwards, you'll begin a training period. This can include a range of activities, such as watching

TIPS FOR SUCCESS

Ensure you're career in retail gets off to a stellar start by following these tips to success:

Be on time: A retail operation is going to open whether you show up for work on time or not. By being late you put work on other colleagues and you begin to establish a poor reputation for yourself as being unreliable. Being on time means you're serious about your job, and you recognize the responsibility is important.

Appropriate workplace behavior: In retail you'll encounter all kinds of customers. Some will be demanding, some will be needy, others will be pushy. No matter how they treat you and no matter what they say to you, you must always remain professional and exhibit appropriate workplace behavior. Avoid getting into arguments with customers, and if you feel you can't handle a situation, call a manager.

Show initiative by asking questions: You'll have a job review after a few months on the job and then you'll have them on a yearly basis. But that doesn't mean you need to wait for feedback on your performance. Ask a manager how you are doing, what skills you could improve, and ways for you to keep learning.

Acing your annual review: At least one time a year your job performance will be evaluated. By asking questions throughout the year and seeking out feedback, you can show improvement over time and exhibit initiative to keep growing in your role.

training videos, participate in training exercises, reading and completing worksheets, shadowing an experienced retail professional, or listening to presentations by your supervisor or store management.

The training is designed to get you familiar with the store's products so you can be knowledgeable with customers and to help you sell effectively if you'll be in a sales position. It It

As part of your new-hire training, you will learn the ins and outs of your store's register system, the processes for product inventory, how you are expected to interact with customers, and more.

Each store also has its own series of steps for cashing out customers and for opening and closing each night. These can vary greatly from store to store and are one of the first things you will likely learn on a new job.

also covers the store procedures for everything from when new merchandise arrives, how it is priced, and when it is put on display to handling special orders, operating the cash register, and the processes for opening or closing the store. Customer service will also be addressed. Since the retail industry is all about getting products into the hands of consumers, dealing with customers is an essential part of the industry, and is crucial for a store's success. You'll likely undergo significant training on customer service.

Career Advancement

Retail is an industry with great opportunities for you to grow professionally. You may begin your career as a sales person who assists customers with their needs. But, for those with ambition, dedication, and a strong work ethic, you can be promoted to positions that carry more responsibility and authority. Many sales people move up to manager positions, where you can be part of a management team responsible for developing sales people and hitting quarterly or annual sales goals. Other leadership positions might include visual merchandiser, sales manager, merchandise buyer, and more.

In an industry that drives the American economy, and with stores in nearly every single town in the country, big and small, there are opportunities for you to excel in the field of retail and to carve out a career for yourself.

GLOSSARY

assertiveness Confidence in behavior or style.

attentive Thinking about or watching something carefully.

competitor Someone who is trying to win or do better than others, especially in business or sports.

consumer A person who spends money to buy products.

consumer behavior A person's behavior as they browse, shop and select products, which many businesses attempt to analyze and predict.

display To put a product where people can see it; also refers to a window display.

e-commerce Buying and selling that happens online.

entrepreneur A person who starts a business, often assuming some amount of financial risk.

franchise The right to sell a company's goods or services in a particular area.

interpersonal Communication that occurs between two people.

mannequin A figure shaped like a human body that is used for displaying clothes or other products.

marketing The activities that are involved in making people aware of a company's products and encouraging them to buy the product, which occur in many spheres, including at retail locations.

non-disclosure agreement Documentation an employee is required to sign promising not to give away sensitive information, especially to a business's competitors.

persistence A quality that allows someone to continue doing something or trying to do something even though it is difficult or opposed by other people.

policy Management or procedure based primarily on material interest.

promotion Something done (such as advertising) to make customers aware of something and increase its popularity and sales.

retailer A person or business that sells products to consumers.

stock The supply of goods available for sale in a store.

traffic The amount of people who pass through a certain place or travel in a certain way.

vocation The work that a person does or should be doing.

American Booksellers Association
333 Westchester Avenue, Suite S202
White Plains, NY 10604
(800) 637-0037
Website: http://www.bookweb.org
The American Booksellers Association provides relevant programs as well as educational opportunities, information, business products, and services to book sellers.

American Management Association
(877) 566-9441
E-mail: customerservice@amanet.org
Website: http://www.amanet.org
The American Management Association has been a world leader in providing professional development to individuals, organizations, and government agencies who need advanced education in leadership, management, coaching, and more.

American Marketing Association
130 E. Randolph Street, 22nd Floor
Chicago, IL 60601
(800) AMA-1150
Website: https://www.ama.org
The American Marketing Association provides leadership, best practices, and resources for all professionals working in the marketing field.

American Specialty Toy Retailing Association
432 N. Clark Street, Suite #305
Chicago, IL 60654
(312) 222-0984
Website: http://www.astratoy.org
The American Specialty Toy Retailing Association (ASTRA)
    provides quality products that help children have fun,
    achieve success, and lead happy, healthy lives.

Consumer Electronics Association
1919 South Eads Street
Arlington, VA 22202
(866) 858-1555
Website: http://www.cta.tech
CTA is the industry authority on market research, con-
    sumer surveys, legislative and regulatory news,
    engineering standards, training resources, and more for
    those who develop, manufacture, and sell electronic
    products.

National Retail Federation
1101 New York Ave NW
Washington, DC 20005
(800) 673-4692
Website: https://nrf.com
NRF is the world's largest retail trade association. The group
    represents all types of stores, including discount and
    department stores, home goods and specialty stores,
    grocers, wholesalers, chain restaurants, and online
    retailers.

Retail Council of Canada
1881 Yonge Street, Suite 800
Toronto, ON M4S 3C4
Canada
(416) 922-6678
http://www.retailcouncil.org
The Retail Council of Canada represents 45,000 store
fronts throughout the retail industry, including department, specialty, discount, and independent stores, and
online merchants. The council strives to be an authori-
tative voice for the Canadian retail industry.

Websites

Because of the changing number of Internet links, Rosen
Publishing has developed an online list of websites related to
the subject of this book. This site is updated regularly. Please
use this link to access this list:

http://www.rosenlinks.com/JOBS/retail

FOR FURTHER READING

Dunne, Patrick M., Robert F. Lusch and James R. Carver. *Retailing.* Cinncinnati, OH: South-Western College/West Publishing, 2010.

Ensaff, Najoud. *Retail Careers.* Mankato, MN: Amicus, 2010.

Easterling, Cynthia R., Ellen L. Flottman, Marian H. Jernigan, and Best ES Wuest. *Merchandising Mathematics for Retailing.* New York, NY: Prenice Hall, 2012.

Glaser, Jason. *Careers in Online Retailing.* New York, NY: Rosen Publishing Group, 2014.

Grose, Virginia. *Basic Fashion Management 01: Fashion Merchandising.* New York, NY: AVA Publishing, 2011.

Rooney, Anne. *In the Workplace: Retail.* Twickenham, United Kingdom: MMS Gold, 2010.

Shaw, David. *Fashion Buying: From Trend Forecasting to Shop Floor.* New York, NY: Fairchild Books, 2013.

Wilkes, Donald, and Viola Hamilton-Wilkes. *Teen Guide Job Search: Ten Easy Steps to Your Future.* Bloomington, IN: iUniverse, Inc., 2006.

Yate, Martin. *Knock'em Dead Job Interview: How to Turn Job Interviews into Job Offers.* Avon, MA: Adams Media, 2012.

Yates, Julia, and Donna Gustavsen. *The Fashion Careers Guidebook: A Guide to Every Career in the Fashion Industry and How to Get It.* Barron's Educational Series: Hauppauge, NY, 2011.

BIBLIOGRAPHY

Bureau of Labor Statistics. "Retail Sales Workers."
December 17, 2015. Retrieved February 1, 2016 (http://
www.bls.gov/ooh/sales/retail-sales-workers.htm#tab-1).

Campusexplorer.com. "7 Best Study Tips for College
Students." Retrieved February 9, 2016 (http://www.
campusexplorer.com/college-advice-tips/2DF9E34D/
7-Best-Study-Tips-for-College-Students).

Careerbuilder.com. "Associate Buyer – Retail." Posted
January 13, 2016. (http://www.careerbuilder.com/job-
seeker/jobs/jobdetails.aspx?APath=2.31.0.0.0&job_did=J3
G5NK6VFD5458QFJ5D&showNewJDP=yes&IPath=ILK
V0N).

Careerbuilder.com. "Visual Merchandiser: Job Description."
February 2, 2016. Retrieved February 3, 2016 (http://
www.careerbuilder.com/jobseeker/jobs/job.detailsaspx?A
Path=2.21.0.0.0&job_did=J3K2MN79K4C7YQ6HM9V&s
howNewJDP=yes&IPath=JRKV0B).

Connecticut Technical High School System. "Fashion
Merchandising and Entrepreneurship Course Sequence."
Retrieved February 9, 2016 (http://www.cttech.org/
central/technical-offerings/fashion-techl.htm).

Connecticut Technical High School System. "Trade/
Technology Clusters." Retrieved February 9, 2016 (http://
www.cttech.org/central/technical-offerings/index.
htm#marketing).

Dachis, Adam. "What's Expected of Me on the First Day of a
New Job?" Lifehacker.com, October 23, 2012. Retrieved
February 9, 2016 (http://lifehacker.com/5954001/
whats-expected-of-me-on-the-first-day-of-a-new-job).

Martin, Emmie. "Why One Executive Says Your Cover Letter
Is More Important Than Your Résumé." Businessinsider.

com, September 22, 2014. Retrieved February 3, 2016 (http://www.businessinsider.com/ why-cover-letters-are-important-2014-9).

Mesa Community College. "Certificate of Completion in Alteration Specialist." Retrieved February 9, 2016 (https://www.mesacc.edu/programs/course-sequences/ alteration-specialist-ccl).

Retailinudstry.about.com. "Personal Shopper Job Description." December 16, 2014. Retrieved February 3, 2016 (http://retailindustry.about.com/od/ retailjobscareers/p/personalshopper.htm)

Targetjobs.com.uk. "Retail Manager: Job Description." Retrieved February 1, 2016 (https://targetjobs.co.uk/ careers-advice/ job-descriptions/27885 1-retail-manager-job-description).

Targetcareers.co.uk. "What types of jobs and employers are there in retail, buying and fashion?" Retrieved February 9, 2016 (https://targetcareers.co.uk/career-sectors/ retail-buying-and-fashion/150-what-types-of-jobs-and-employers-are-there-in-retail-buying-and-fashion).

Themuse.com. "How to Write a Cover Letter: 31 Tips You Need to Know." Retrieved February 1, 2016 (https:// www.themuse.com/advice/how-to-write-a-cover-letter-31-tips-you-need-to-know).

Tkaczyk, Christopher. "20 great Workplaces in Retail." *Fortune*, November 19, 2014. Retrieved February 9, 2016 (http://fortune.com/2014/11/19/20-great-workplaces -in-retail).

INDEX

About the Author

Laura La Bella is a writer who put herself through college by working in retail. She is the author of more than thirty-five nonfiction children's books. She lives in Rochester, N.Y., with her husband and sons.

Photo Credits

Cover, p. 1 (figure) Yuri Arcurs/DigitalVision/Getty Images; cover, p. 1 (background), interior pages, back cover Tony Tremblay/E+/Getty Images; p. 5 Joos Mind/The Image Bank/ Getty Images; p. 8 Tom Pennington/Getty Images; pp. 10-11, 50, 55 Bloomberg/Getty Images; pp. 12-13 Jon Riley/The Image Bank/Getty Images; pp. 14-15 Comstock/Stockbyte/ Getty Images; pp. 18-19, 45, 46-47 Justin Sullivan/Getty Images; p. 21 Thomas EyeDesign/E+/Getty Images; pp. 22-23 Andy Cross/The Denver Post/Getty Images; pp. 26-27 Dmitry Kalinovsky/Shutterstock.com; p. 33 JGI/Blend Images/Getty Images; p. 37 alvarez/E+/Getty Images; pp. 38-39 Hero Images/ Getty Images; pp. 40-41 Alex Wong/Getty Images; p. 49 Scott Olson/Getty Images; p. 57 Leland Bobbe/The Image Bank/ Getty Images; p. 59 Sam Diephuis/Blend Images/Getty Images; pp. 64-65 Blend Images-Erik Isakson/Brand X Pictures/Getty Images; p. 67 fotofrog/E+/Getty Images; p. 68 ML Harris/The Image Bank/Getty Images

Designer: Nicole Russo; Editor: Philip Wolny;
Photo Researcher: Philip Wolny